P9-BZS-168

Running Free

AMERICA'S WILD HORSES

Written and Photographed by

FRANK STAUB

Enslow Publishers, Inc.
40 Industrial Road
Box 398
Berkeley Heights, NJ 07922
USA

http://www.enslow.com

For Kathy

"*. . . Congress finds and declares that wild free-roaming horses and burros are living symbols of the historic and pioneer spirit of the West; [and] that they contribute to the diversity of life forms within the Nation and enrich the lives of the American people . . .* "

—From Public Law 92-195, "The Wild Free-Roaming Horses and Burros Act," signed by President Richard M. Nixon, December 15, 1971.

Acknowledgements—The author would like to thank the following for their help with this book: Assurance Home, Roswell, New Mexico; Black Hills Wild Horse Sanctuary, Hot Springs, South Dakota; Chad Grizzle; Chincoteague Volunteer Fire Department, Virginia; Custer State Park, South Dakota; Grayson Highlands State Park, Virginia; Lifesavers, Inc., Lancaster, California; Lynda Konrad; National Park Service; National Zoo Conservation and Research Center, Front Royal, Virginia; Nevada Department of Agriculture; Oatman, Arizona; Peaceful Valley Donkey Rescue, Tehachapi, California; Return to Freedom, Lompoc, California; US Bureau of Land Management; US Fish and Wildlife Service; US Forest Service; Wild Horse Sanctuary, Shingleton, California.

Library of Congress Cataloging-in-Publication Data

Staub, Frank J.

    Running free : America's wild horses / by Frank Staub.

       p. cm. — (Prime)

    Includes bibliographical references and index.

    ISBN 0-7660-2670-1

    1. Wild horses—United States—Miscellanea—Juvenile literature. I. Title. II. Series.

    SF360.3.U6S73 2006

    599.665'5—dc22

                      2005033995

Printed in the United States of America

10 9 8 7 6 5 4 3 2 1

The photographs in this book were taken by the author, © *Frank J. Staub, in the following locations:*

Cover Photos: Mount Rogers, Virginia (back, top); near Reno, Nevada (back, bottom); Northwestern Colorado near Maybell (front).

Interior Photos: Assateague Island, Virginia, 20, 36-37; crossing from Assateague Island in Virginia to Chincoteague Island, 40-41; Assurance Home, Roswell, New Mexico, 42; Black Hills Wild Horse Sanctuary, Hot Springs, South Dakota, 1, 3, 6-7, 14, 26-27, 35, 44-48; Cumberland Island, Georgia, 8-9, 21 (top), 34; Custer State Park, South Dakota, 10-11 (inset); farm in Georgia, 19 (circle and far right); Hagerman Fossil Beds National Monument, Idaho, 12, 16; Mount Rogers, Virginia, 29, 33 (bottom); National Zoo Research and Conservation Center, Virginia, 18-19 (lower left); Northwestern Colorado near Maybell, 4-5, 38-39; Red Rock Canyon, Nevada, 10-11; Return to Freedom, Lompoc, California, 2, 22-23, 24-25, 25 (top right), 32 (both); Shackleford Banks, North Carolina, 13; Wild Horse Sanctuary, Shingleton, California, 21 (oval), 25 (circle), 28, 30-31, 33 (top).

Additional Photos: Corel Corporation, branches on cover and pages 1–2.

CONTENTS

Are there still wild horses?

Imagine a herd of wild horses, kicking up dust as they thunder across an open plain. It's a classic symbol of the old American West. And it's a scene we can enjoy today. Wild horses still run free in almost every western state. Most live in areas with few trees where they can graze on grasses and other plants. Water holes are often few and far between. So are the towns, for this is ranching country. Most of America's wild horses share their home with cowboys and cattle, wildlife, and various other users of our public lands.

Where did today's wild horses first come from?

*F*armers, ranchers, miners, soldiers, and practically everyone else who lived, worked, and traveled in America before there were cars and trucks used horses. America's dependence on the horse began with the early Spanish explorers. They brought small, tough horses to what is now Mexico during the 1500s. Native Americans got horses from the Spaniards and spread them northward to the Rocky Mountains. Settlers from other countries brought additional horse breeds that were usually bigger than those of the Spaniards.

As time went by, some of the horses escaped and wandered off into the wilderness. Others were set free when their owners didn't need them anymore. The ancestors of these strays came from many lands, just like the people who had owned them. That's why most of western America's wild horses today are a mixture of different horse breeds. Still, in the American West, where most wild horses live, they're all called "mustangs," from a Spanish word for "stray" or "stranger."

Are there any wild horses in the east?

Yes. Wild horses live on several islands along the eastern coast of the United States: Cumberland Island in Georgia (as shown here), Shackleford Banks and Currituck Island in North Carolina, and Assateague Island in Virginia and Maryland. Some also dwell inland, on Mount Rogers in southwestern Virginia.

Legend says that some of the island horses' ancestors swam ashore hundreds of years ago from Spanish ships that sank in the Atlantic Ocean just offshore. But most were probably strays that once belonged to east coast farmers. Over the years, people released additional horses onto the islands.

Many of the wild horses on America's eastern islands are small—so small that people call them ponies. Whether or not a horse is called a pony has to do with its height. A horse's height is measured by the number of "hands" from the ground to the top of its withers (the highest part of a horse's back, at the base of the neck between the shoulders). One hand equals four inches, or roughly the width of a man's hand. A pony is 14.2 hands high or shorter.

The island horses may have inherited their pony size from the short horses ridden by the early Spaniards. Or a poor diet may have stunted their growth, since the grasses on the islands are low in nutrients. It may also be that small horses survive hardships better than larger horses—a small body needs less food and water.

Are America's wild burros related to horses?

Burros belong to a group of strong, sure-footed, hardy members of the horse family called asses. Burros are much smaller than most true horses. East of the Mississippi River, people call them donkeys. But in the west, "burro," the Spanish word for "donkey," is more common. People have used burros to ride, carry big loads, pull plows, and do other sorts of heavy labor.

Spanish missionaries brought the first burros to the American Southwest during the 1500s. Later, miners used burros to haul their gear and carry the rocks that contained the minerals they prospected for, such as gold and silver. When the mining operations slowed down, the miners freed their faithful burros. Some of America's wild burros also descended from the pack animals used by sheep herders.

Burros need much less water than horses do. They can also eat rougher, dryer plants. This explains how America's wild burros can survive in the dry deserts of Arizona, California, and Nevada. A small population of wild burros also lives in Custer State Park, South Dakota.

Burros are smaller than horses with bigger ears, narrower hooves, and short, stiff manes.

Have there always been horses in North America?

*N*orth America is actually where horses first appeared. About fifty-five million years ago, an animal similar to the small tapirs now living in Central and South America gave rise to the first animal that could be called a horse. Its legs, neck, snout, and tail were short.

These horses lived in the forests and swamps covering much of North America then. They could hide among the trees from wolves, mountain lions, and other predators. But over time, the environment changed. Grasslands replaced forests and swamps. Now the horses had to constantly watch for danger and run away when threatened. The biggest, fastest horses, with the best hearing and sharpest eyesight, had the best chance to escape. These traits helped the horses live longer and have more young, which were usually fast and alert like their parents. In this way, the horse slowly changed into the large, swift animal of the plains we know today. This process of evolution took many millions of years.

This skeleton (left) is from a primitive horse. The modern horse (right) evolved about 1.67 million years ago.

How did horses become so well suited to life on the plains?

Developing long, powerful legs was just one of the ways horses adapted to life on the open, grassy plains. Their nostrils and lungs grew large, allowing them to suck in lots of air while running. Horses once had three toes on each foot, which was helpful on marshy ground. Over time the center toe developed into a single hard hoof, which provides protection on rocky ground and is more suited to running fast on the hard plains.

In addition, as grasslands replaced the forests and swamps, the horse changed from a leaf-eating animal into a grass-eater. It developed a long jaw with special teeth for grinding up tough wild grasses. Its eyes moved high above its jaws. Because of this, a horse can spot an approaching predator while grazing without lifting its head. And as the horse's legs grew long, its neck become long too, allowing it to reach the ground to eat. A long neck also gave the horse a higher view to look about for enemies.

What happened to the ancient horses?

This fossil includes the jawbone and vertebrae of a primitive horse.

*R*oughly 10,000 to 12,000 years ago, all the horses in North America disappeared. But why? Did they run out of food? Did the climate change so much that they could not adjust? Did a deadly disease wipe them out? Some scientists think hunting by Native Americans played a role in killing off many of America's prehistoric animals, including horses.

But long before ancient horses vanished from North America, some had wandered across a wide bridge of land that once connected Alaska with Asia. This land bridge existed because sea levels were much lower than they are today. From Asia, the horses spread to Europe. These were the horses that ancient people in eastern Europe and central Asia first caught, tamed, and rode about 6,000 years ago. And their descendants include the horses that the Spanish explorers eventually brought back to North America in the 1500s.

Evidence exists that today's wild mustangs are the same species as some of the prehistoric horses that once roamed those same lands. Some scientists say this proves that the mustang is a native North American animal, which was simply reintroduced after a long absence. Others argue that America's wild horses are feral. A feral animal is not the same as a wild native species. Rather, it is a domestic animal that now lives in the wild.

Do all horses now have domestic ancestors?

During the late 1800s, a Russian explorer named Przewalski ("pur-zhu-VALL-skee") found small wild horses called "takhis" in Mongolia. The Mongolians considered them a nuisance and killed off many of them. Fortunately, some takhis had been protected in zoos and wild animal parks. Today the offspring of those captive animals are being returned to Mongolia's grasslands. The Mongolian government has declared the takhi a national symbol.

The tarpan was a small wild horse that ran free in Europe and western Russia. By the late 1800s, all the tarpans had been killed as people turned the horses' wild homes into farms. But before the tarpan went extinct, some had mated with domestic horses. Now people breed horses with tarpan blood to produce offspring as much like the original tarpans as possible.

The short horses that the early Spaniards brought to America had certain characteristics like takhis and tarpans: a small body, dark legs with ring-like leg stripes, and a thin dark dorsal stripe from mane to tail. These traits occasionally show up in mustangs. Some mustangs also have short hairs at the top of the tail, just as some takhis do.

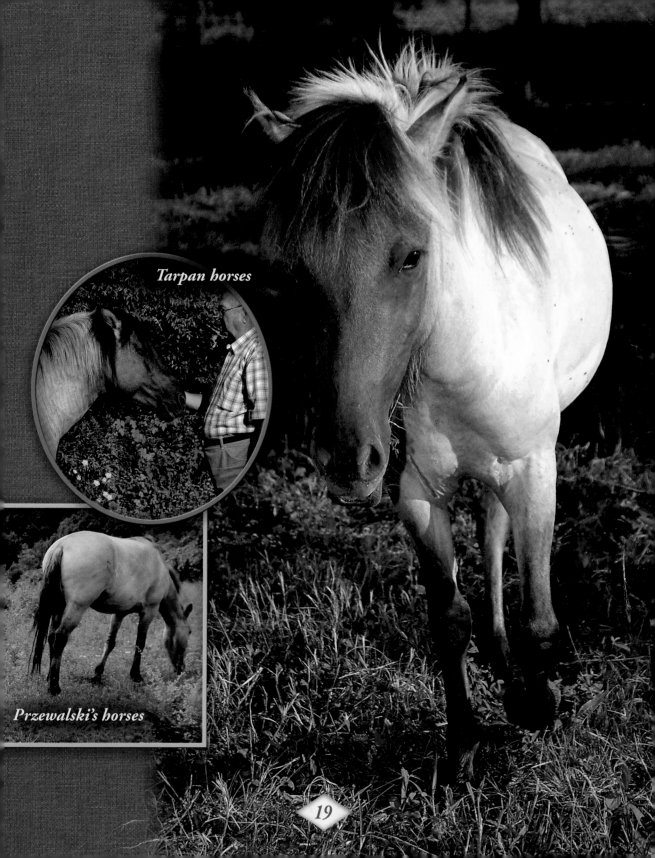

Tarpan horses

Przewalski's horses

Are wild horses good for the environment?

ild horses provide many benefits. For example, when they eat certain plants, the seeds come out in their waste. Sprouts often shoot up quickly from these seeds, because horse droppings are full of the nutrients that plants need to grow.

Wild horses break the winter ice on meadows and ponds, exposing food and water for themselves as well as for other animals. Horses also dig holes in dry ponds during periods of low rainfall. The holes fill with water from below the surface, which may be the only source of moisture for the area's wildlife. Interestingly, some birds will "groom" horses, eating insects and other material on the horse's body. And after a horse dies, its large body provides plenty of meals for scavengers such as coyotes, vultures, foxes, and crows. As a horse carcass rots, it also releases nutrients back into the soil.

Wild horses pose some problems, too. For example, too many horses can lead to overgrazing and trampling of vegetation. This can affect the density and diversity of the plants and animals in the environment.

Do wild horses live alone or in groups?

A harem stallion keeps watch while his mares graze.

$\mathcal{M}$ost wild horses live in small bands. A harem band is usually made up of a single stallion (adult male) and anywhere from one to twenty mares (adult females) plus their offspring. The harem stallion will not let other stallions come near the mares in his band. He watches for danger and protects his band when trouble arises. But one of the older mares acts as the band's leader, deciding where to graze and when to visit a water hole. The lead mare finds the band a sheltered canyon or patch of trees to get out of the wind in a storm.

After leaving a harem band, many young stallions join a bachelor band. Bachelors aren't old enough or strong enough to have harems. But sometimes a bachelor steals mares from a harem band, or even takes over a whole harem. In this way the harem stallion may change. But the mares often stay together throughout their lives.

Does living in a band help horses survive in the wild?

A harem stallion chases off a bachelor trying to bother the harem mares.

*L*ife is easier and safer for horses that travel in bands instead of alone. A band of horses, with many sets of eyes and ears, has a better chance of detecting a predator than a single horse does. Also, predators are more likely to attack a lone animal than a group of animals.

Insect pests, especially biting flies, are another enemy that horses handle better when they live together. The swishing tails of horses standing side by side and facing in opposite directions keeps the bugs away from each other's faces. Furthermore, digging for water in the bottom of an empty pond goes faster when many hooves share the labor. And walking through deep snow isn't as hard when others help clear a trail. Horses that are not in bands are often the first to die during the winter when food is scarce, especially if they are young and inexperienced.

How far does a band of wild horses roam?

*E*ach band has a home range over which it wanders. The home ranges of different bands may overlap, because the horses in a band do allow other horses to enter their home range.

A home range has no definite boundaries. Its size varies from season to season and year to year. When heavy rains spur a lot of plant growth, a band may have all the food it needs within just a few square miles. But dry years produce fewer plants and cause some water holes to dry up. Then a band may have to travel within a home range of hundreds of square miles to find enough to eat and drink. Home ranges are also larger in winter, when thick layers of snow cover the grass. Then mustangs must travel far and wide in search of food.

What is a wild foal's first year of life like?

Mare and foal often stand side by side while nursing.

Foals, or young horses less than one year old, are born in the spring when there are plenty of fresh green plants to eat. Most mares give birth to one foal at a time. Twins are rare.

The timing of a foal's birth is important. If it is born too early in the spring, a late-season snowstorm could kill it. Foals born too late may not have enough time to grow big and strong before winter.

Pregnant mares usually wander off alone to give birth. A newborn foal weighs about 65 to 85 pounds, and may gain a pound a day during the first two months of life. Thick fluffy hair keeps it warm. Within an hour or two after it's born, the foal is up on its feet and walking. A mare keeps other horses away from her newborn to protect it, and possibly so it won't be confused about who its mother is.

At first, a foal's only food is its mother's milk. After a few weeks, it starts to graze. A growing foal spends more and more time wandering away from its mother to graze, play with other foals, and explore. As it grows, the amount of grass in its diet increases, though it may keep nursing until it becomes a yearling (a horse in its second year of life).

Do young horses stay in the band they were born in?

When a young horse reaches sexual maturity, when it can have a foal of its own, it usually leaves the band of its birth. For a filly, or young female, this usually occurs when it is about two years old. It usually leaves on its own to join another harem, or rarely it may be forced away by its mother or the harem stallion. A colt, or young male, reaches sexual maturity at about two or three years of age. Then the harem stallion forces it to leave. A colt on its own usually joins a bachelor band.

Making the young leave the harem band may seem cruel. But this may be nature's way to prevent inbreeding or mating with relatives. An inbred foal from a mother and father that are blood relatives is more likely to have health problems than offspring from parents that are not related.

How do wild horses "talk" to each other?

Flehman display

Snaking

Champing

Mutual grooming

*H*orses snort when they sense danger, squeal when they defend themselves, and "neigh" or "whinny" to call out to others. We can only guess the meaning of many of the sounds horses make. But we do know that a horse usually answers only sounds made by members of its own band.

A horse also expresses itself through behavior. It may shake its head when stressed, or toss its head back and possibly flatten its ears against its neck to show anger. To signal an adult not to hurt it, a foal will open and close its mouth in a gesture known as champing. And stallions herd their mares by stretching their necks and lowering their heads, a behavior called snaking. Mutual grooming through soothing nibbles helps remove burrs and loose hairs, and also helps strengthen the relationship between horses.

Scent helps horses communicate, too. A mother and her foal recognize each other by smell. The odor of a droppings pile lets other horses know who was there. A mare gives off a certain scent which signals that she is ready to mate. In response, a stallion exhibits a flehman display—he lifts his head, curls his top lip back, and inhales deeply to take in her scent.

Do wild horses ever fight?

Stallions may fight over food, water, and mares. When a bachelor tries to steal a mare, the harem stallion usually chases him away. If the bachelor doesn't flee, the two horses may face each other and paw the ground, or show other aggressive behavior as a warning. Actual fights are usually short but violent, with a lot of biting, kicking, and pushing.

Aggression between band members sometimes occurs. A lead mare may force another horse to get out of her way. Or if a foal lags behind, an adult may give it a nip. Colts often have play fights, biting each other lightly and rising up on their back legs the way fighting stallions do. Young stallions in bachelor bands also kick and bite to play. This is good practice—and allows them to judge each other's strength for the future, when they'll compete for mares.

While play fights among bachelors (left) rarely result in injuries, a fight between a harem stallion and a mare-stealing bachelor (above) can be violent.

Have people caused problems for wild horses?

More and more roads, houses, and people have spread into the areas where wild horses once lived.

*D*uring the 1800s, thousands of settlers moved west. Many of them raised cattle. At first the cattle ranchers didn't mind the wild horses that freely roamed the range. They tamed some of them for riding, and for pulling wagons and plows. They even released some of their own domestic horses to breed with the mustangs, in hopes of "improving" the wild herd. But during the 1900s, as ranchers put more and more cattle on the land, they no longer wanted horses eating the grass and drinking the water that would otherwise go to their cows.

Many ranchers hired "mustangers" to help capture the horses. Unfortunately, some of their methods could be very cruel. And after being caught, the terrified creatures were sometimes crammed into trucks and hauled long distances without food or water.

Most captured horses ended up as chicken feed or pet food. Hide buyers also bought some. Some became rodeo "broncos," while others became cavalry mounts in World War I and other conflicts.

At the beginning of the 1900s, the wild horse population in the west was about two million. By 1926, their numbers had been cut in half.

How was the slaughter stopped?

any concerned citizens were outraged by the mustangs' plight. But none had a greater impact than Velma Johnston, also known as Wild Horse Annie. Johnston saw blood dripping from a truck full of horses. She followed the truck to a slaughterhouse and witnessed the horrible way the animals were treated. She began a campaign to convince the government to protect America's wild horses and burros. In 1959, Congress passed the "Wild Horse Annie Act," which gave the horses some protection.

Catching wild horses was still legal, though. By 1970 the population of wild horses in the west had plunged to about 17,000 by some estimates. The public became outraged. Newspapers and magazines published articles about it. Children wrote to their senators and representatives, who received more letters about the mustangs' plight than any other issue except the Vietnam War. Finally, in 1971 Congress passed the Wild Free-Roaming Horses and Burros Act, making it illegal to capture, kill, or harass wild horses and burros.

To keep the number of wild horses from growing too large, the government also started a program called Adopt-a-Horse. Each year the government gathers thousands of wild mustangs and offers them to the public for adoption.

When the mustang population grows too large, the government holds a gather. Here, a helicopter herds some of the animals toward a trained "Judas horse" (with rope and halter) that leads them into an enclosure. Later they will be offered to the public for adoption.

Are there too many wild horses in the east?

The islands where most eastern wild horses live are small. Scientists are concerned that if there are too many wild horses, they will eat up all the food and die of starvation. Also, too many horses grazing and trampling vegetation can interfere with the islands' natural environments and make it hard for plants and other animals to survive.

On Assateague Island in Maryland and Virginia, both auctioning and birth control are used to help control the wild horse population. On the Maryland side, mares are shot with a small dart that contains a contraceptive. The dart doesn't hurt the animals, but the contraceptive keeps them from becoming pregnant for one year.

The ponies on the Virginia side are owned by the Chincoteague Volunteer Fire Company. Each July, they round up 100 or more of the ponies and coax them to swim across a narrow channel to Chincoteague Island. There the foals are auctioned off to raise money for the local fire department.

Are wild horses hard to adopt and tame?

You must be at least 18 to adopt a wild horse from the government. But a parent or guardian may adopt and allow a younger family member to care for the animal. An adopter is required to have a proper truck or trailer to take the horse home. They also must have the right kind of facilities for keeping the horse: enough space, suitable fences, and adequate shelter. And an adopted animal may not be used as a rodeo bucking bronco or treated inhumanely in any way. For the first year after a horse is adopted, the government still legally owns it. Then they will release the title of ownership, but only if the adopter has properly cared for the animal.

Owning a horse can be expensive—often more than $1000 a year. The animal must have proper food and veterinary care. There may be the cost of renting a corral and stall as well as buying a saddle and bridle. Unfortunately, too many people who adopt a wild horse don't know what they're getting into. These animals really are wild. Gentling them for riding or working takes a lot of time, patience, and kindness—especially with older horses. It may require attending a horse taming class or workshop, or hiring a trainer.

Also, an owner must never forget that horses are social animals. They need companionship. A horse kept by itself without any other horses needs a lot of human attention, gentle touching, and kind words. Otherwise it may become depressed or develop other problems.

What is the future of wild horses in America?

Many ranchers claim their work is hard enough without mustangs eating acres of grass that could feed their cattle and drinking gallons of water in an area where water is scarce. Some also complain about mustangs breaking down fences and stealing domestic mares from corrals. Other people argue that there are too many cattle, not horses, on public lands. After all, they say, millions of cattle currently use America's public lands compared with only thirty to forty thousand wild horses. The laws that protect wild horses are subject to constant debate. They have been adjusted in various ways over time, and it is possible that they could change again.

It is impossible to predict what the future holds for America's wild horses. But one thing is certain: when one sees a mustang running free, unconfined by fences and ropes, it is easy to understand how wild horses have become such powerful symbols of the spirit of freedom. And that freedom gives wild horses their special appeal as living American legends.

Glossary

bachelor band—A group of young stallions that do not yet have their own harem bands.

burro—A type of donkey that is common in the western United States; from the Spanish word for donkey.

colt—A young male horse.

feral—A domestic animal that now lives in the wild.

filly—A young female horse.

flehman display—A behavior in which a stallion takes in the scent of a mare that is ready to mate.

foal—A horse that is less than one year old.

hand—Measure used for a horse's height. One hand equals four inches, about the width of a man's hand.

harem band—A group of horses usually made up of a single stallion and one to twenty mares plus their offspring.

home range—The area that a band lives and travels within to find food and water.

lead mare—An older mare who acts as a harem band leader.

mare—An adult female horse.

mustang—A type of horse found on the western American plains; from a Spanish word for stray or stranger.

pony—A horse that is 14.2 hands high or shorter.

Przewalski's horse—A species of small wild horse living in Mongolia that Russian explorer Przewalski found in the late 1800s; also called "takhi."

snaking—A behavior in which a stallion stretches its neck and lowers its head in order to herd its mares.

stallion—An adult male horse.

tapir—A small mammal with hooves and an elongated snout that lives in Central and South America.

tarpan—A species of small wild horse that once lived in Europe and western Russia.

withers—The highest point on a horse's back, at the base of the neck between the shoulders.

yearling—A horse in its second year of life, at least one but not yet two years old.

Further Reading

Books

Penny, Malcolm. *Wild Horses*. Austin, Tex.: Raintree Steck-Vaughn, 2002.

Peterson, Cris. *Wild Horses: Black Hills Sanctuary*. Honesdale, Pa.: Boyds Mills Press, 2003.

Swanson, Diane. *Welcome to the World of Wild Horses*. Vancouver: Whitecap Books, 2002.

Vogel, Julia. *Wild Horses*. Chanhassen, Minn.: NorthWord Press, 2004.

Internet Addresses

Assateague's Wild Horses
http://www.nps.gov/archive/asis/horses.htm

Black Hills Wild Horse Sanctuary
http://www.wildmustangs.com

Bureau of Land Management National Wild Horse and Burro Program
http://www.wildhorseandburro.blm.gov

Wild Horses: An American Romance
http://net.unl.edu/artsFeat/wildhorses

Index